This book is a gift to

_____

_____

_____

FROM

_____

DATE

For the eyes of the Lord are on the
righteous and His ears are attentive
to their prayer. 1 Peter 3:12

C
O
N
V
E
R
S
A
T
I
O
N
S

with God

Teens Pray

CONCORDIA PUBLISHING HOUSE · SAINT LOUIS

BY EDWARD GRUBE

Teens
Pray

Preface

A survey of students revealed this about their prayer practices:

* Most students pray for themselves, their family, and friends.

* The four times when students pray most often are when they go to bed, at mealtime, when they're in trouble, and when they're confused.

* The majority of students made up their own prayers or used a traditional prayer like the Lord's Prayer or Come, Lord, Jesus.

Does God listen to young believers as they pray? How can we imperfect humans dare to approach our holy God? Conversations with Him would be impossible were it not for Jesus, sent by God to redeem sinners. Jesus' suffering, death, and resurrection took away our sins and made it possible to approach God in full confidence of His loving attention.

God not only invites us to pray, He commands it. Here are some things God tells us in the Bible about prayer:

Seek the LORD while He may be found;
call on Him while He is near.
Isaiah 55:6

Ask and it will be given to you; seek and you will find; knock and the door will be opened to you.
Matthew 7:7

Do not be anxious about anything,
but in everything, by prayer and petition,
with thanksgiving, present your requests to God.
Philippians 4:6

God's Word makes it quite clear. He wants us to pray. But what does He want us to pray about? God's people are free to talk to Him about anything. In praying about spiritual matters, we are bold. As we pray for stronger faith or to give God glory through our words and deeds, we're confident that His will and ours are one. When we pray for material or physical matters, we should always conclude with the phrase, ". . . if it is Your will." Sometimes what we want isn't what God wants for us. He knows that some of our desires will hurt us or damage our faith. He would never give anything bad to us, even if we plead for such things.

In what way should prayers be offered? Many people fold or cross their hands. Some people pray privately, while others are comfortable speaking aloud. Others offer prayers by speaking them in their minds; people around them would never guess they are praying.

The Bible has described praying as a lifting up, pouring out, crying, and shouting. Your prayers may be offered however you want to speak to God. This book's subtitle is Conversations with God. The phrase suggests that because Jesus has given you direct access to God, you are free to speak with Him as you speak to people.

What about answers to prayer? God always answers prayer. Sometimes it's a "yes," sometimes a "no." Sometimes it's a "wait awhile." Regardless of the answer, God hears you and cares about what you have to say. This is what the Bible says about the subject:

> Before they call I will answer;
> while they are still speaking
> I will hear. Isaiah 65:24

Be aware that God may answer prayers in unexpected ways. For example, suppose you pray often for a loved one who is sick. Your prayers are sincere. You're confident that God hears your prayers and that He loves your loved one too. But then your loved one dies. Does that mean God didn't answer your prayers? Not at all. God does whatever He wants and whatever is best regardless of what we think. You prayed that your loved one would be healed. And that's what God did. He took your loved one—who had faith in Jesus Christ as his or her Savior—to be with Him in heaven. In heaven, there is no illness or suffering. Only perfect health and happiness. Is there any better healing? You may indeed pray that your loved one gets well here on earth. But this is one of those cases where we must leave it entirely in God's hands—according to His will.

Do you sometimes wonder to whom you should address your prayers? Should you be talking to God the Father, Jesus His Son, or the Holy Spirit? God has a great system for routing prayers. Since He is the Triune God—Father, Son, and Holy Spirit—your prayers always go to the right Person of the Trinity! Don't worry about the address. Your prayers get through! By the way, you may have heard some people praying to saints or the Virgin Mary. Don't do it! You see, sometimes people pray to others because they fear that God will not listen to sinners like themselves. How sad! We know that Jesus took away our sins and gives us free and personal access to God.

For whom should we pray? We're free to pray for ourselves and all other people, even those who don't believe. It is important that you pray for those whose faith is weak or who refuse to believe that Jesus is their Savior while they are living. Among all those for whom you pray, this group is most in need of your conversations with God!

I encourage you to use this book for yourself and for those times when you might be called upon to lead a prayer. Many of the prayers contain blanks where you may fill in the name of an individual for whom you are praying. Other prayers include blanks for specific situations for which you may be praying.

I also encourage you to make up your own prayers. Don't worry about word selection, proper grammar, or making mistakes. You see, the Holy Spirit prays with us and for us. In fact, the Holy Spirit is a most thoughtful and generous prayer partner. Take a look at this:

> … the Spirit helps us in our weakness. We do not know what we ought to pray for, but the Spirit Himself intercedes for us with groans that words cannot express. Romans 8:26

Wow! What a privilege it is to pray. Thank God you are free to exercise that privilege. Pray often. Pray confidently. Pray for yourself, your family, your friends, your enemies, and even those you don't know. God loves you. You can speak freely to Him.

Edward Grube

Contents

PREFACE

SICKNESS
> General 17
> Minor 18
> Major 18
> Others 19

SCHOOL MATTERS
> Protection in My School 20
> After Violence Elsewhere 21
> Starting a New School Year 21
> For My School 22
> Ending a School Year 23

GRADES
> When You've Done Your Best 24
> When You Need To Do Better 25
> For Others 25

TESTS
> Preparation 26
> Just Before 27
> Right After 27

EXTRACURRICULAR EVENTS
> Athletics 28
> Music 29
> Drama 30

FORGIVENESS
> For Others 31
> For Self 32

SAD TIMES

When You Are Sad 34

Sad—But Don't Know Why 35

RELATIONSHIPS

Friends 36

Loss of a Friend 37

Male-Female Relationships 38

Parents 41

Brothers/Sisters 43

Teachers 44

TEMPTATIONS

Sexual 45

Cheating 46

Anger 47

Stealing 48

Drugs 49

PEER PRESSURE

To Resist 50

Failure to Resist 51

DRIVING

New Driver's License 52

Before Driving 53

Before Riding Along 53

COURAGE

General 54

In Witnessing 55

Facing Life's Challenges 56

SUCCESS

Personal Success 57

When Others Succeed 59

MISCELLANEOUS PRAYERS FOR OTHERS

Enemies 60

Unbelievers 61

News-Makers 62

DAILY PRAYERS

Sunday 63

Monday 64

Tuesday 64

Wednesday 65

Thursday 65

Friday 66

Saturday 67

BIRTHDAY

Birthday – Self 68

Birthday – Others 69

WORSHIP AND SACRAMENT

Before Worship 70

Before the Lord's Supper 71

After the Lord's Supper 71

SEASONAL

Spring 73

Summer 74

Fall 74

Winter 75

Advent 75

Christmas 76

New Year 77

Lent 77

Easter 78

Ascension Day 79

Pentecost 79

COMMON PRAYERS

The Lord's Prayer 80

PRAYERS FROM LUTHER'S CATECHISM

Morning Prayer 82

Evening Prayer 83

Before Meals 83

After Meals 83

PRAYERS BASED ON THE COMMANDMENTS

1–3 A Good Relationship
with God 84

4 Respect and Obedience 85

5 Loving Others 86

6 Another Prayer About Sex 87

7 Honesty 88

8 Well, Well, Well 89

9–10 Contentment 90

MISCELLANEOUS PRAYERS

Doing God's Will 91

Self-Control 92

Decision-Making 92

Patience 93

For My Country 94

For Times When I'm Too Busy 95

Sickness

I never appreciate my health so much as when I'm sick, Lord. Oh, I don't feel like I'm going to die, and even if I did, I know You would be there. Right now, I'd just like to feel better. As you restore my health, make me a better person too—one who will serve You happily and healthily. I pray in the name of Him who cares for all needs, great and small.   Amen.

MINOR

Lord Jesus, I don't know if I should bother You—after all, hospitals are full of people who need Your healing more than I do. But since You love me enough to suffer pain and die for me, I'm certain You do care. Restore my health so I can serve You and others again. I pray in the name of the One who directed healing for lepers and mobility to the lame.   Amen.

MAJOR

I'm afraid, dear Jesus. You already know just how serious it is, but I have to tell You anyway. I'm afraid of the pain. I'm afraid of the uncertainty about my future. Yes, Jesus, I'm afraid even though You are here for me now and You will be there for me when I go to heaven. I'm afraid of dying. Or maybe it's just that I hope for so much in life that I don't want to miss any of it. You know all about pain and death. You went through it for me. You know about life too; You lived it fully. Now take me through it, heal me, if it is Your will, and comfort me. My hope is in You, Great Physician. Amen.

Insert the name of the one for whom you're praying in the blank.

Heavenly Healer, _____
needs Your care and comfort. Give the doctors
skill and make the medications effective. Give me
whatever I need to help in _____'s
healing and comfort. And while You restore
_____'s health, bring Your healing
to all who suffer, if it is Your will, and lead them
to know that You are their loving Savior. I pray
in the name of the Powerful Servant who healed
thousands on His way to the cross. Amen.

School Matters

Father, just about the time I forget about school violence, it's in the news again. Will it ever be in my classrooms or hallways or cafeteria? I know Lord, that violence is never Your will. Protect us from those who would harm us. Bring Your love to my school and rule in our hearts. I pray in the name of the Lord of peace.

Amen.

AFTER VIOLENCE ELSEWHERE

I'm so sad, dear Jesus, about what happened at _____ school. Help those who are hurt, and comfort their families. Send faithful Christian witnesses to let them know that Your love is stronger than the worst hate and horror. Keep us safe at our school, and send Your Holy Spirit to help us trust You for safety. I pray in the name of the Lord of peace. Amen.

STARTING A NEW SCHOOL YEAR

Lord Jesus, it seems like such a long time— now through the end of the school year. I know that Your will for me is to succeed and be happy. I also know that to be happy and to succeed mean that I need to live the kind of life You expect from Your people. Help me do that, Jesus. Help me to learn that I may serve You and the people You give me to know. Give me old friends and new—all of them who will let me be me—all of them who will respect me for being Yours.

Strengthen me with the desire and self-discipline that I'll need to learn from my teachers, experiences, and books. Make all that I do become one more piece of that person You want me to be.

I know you've heard me. And thanks, in advance, for all those times in the coming year when You will listen to me again. Even when I don't raise my hand! I pray in Your name, faithful Teacher.   Amen.

FOR MY SCHOOL

My friends might laugh if they knew I was praying for my school! It's just one of those things about which most of us rarely pray, dear Jesus. So here I am, praying that my school be a good place to learn and a safe place too. Bless my teachers, especially those who are grouchy, shy, unsure of themselves, and even mean. Use me to help them!

Sometimes the things that happen in my school don't seem very Christian. Help me—and other students—to sort out the temptations and unbiblical information from that which is true. And as I learn many new things, help me find ways to turn that knowledge into action that brings You glory.

Yes, Lord Jesus, help my school. Be there with me, the other students, the faculty, the principal, and other school workers. Lead us to know You better and to grow in ways that testify of Your love for us.   Amen.

Summer vacation! I thought it would never get here, Lord Jesus. You have brought me through another year in school. Thank you for giving me a school and teachers to help me grow. My attitude wasn't always the best this past year. Forgive me for those times when I displeased You—those times when I didn't work up to my potential or when I was disrespectful to teachers and other students. Forgive me for those times when I didn't act like I'm Your child. Strengthen me to fight those sins in the future.

Now, as I think about my vacation days, lead me where You want me to go. Wherever I am, remind me that I belong to You. Without the pressures of classes, I may be tempted to stray from You in my prayer life. I know I need You all the time, not only when school is in session. Stay with me. Keep me close to You. Give me an enjoyable vacation period, and help Me to know more of Your love. I pray in Your name.   Amen.

Grades

Thank You, God, for giving me the desire and ability to learn. My grades reflect the skills, talents, and attitudes with which You have blessed me. Continue to be my Study Partner, empowering me to learn that I may serve You and Your people. Keep me from pride and boasting; make me curious about Your world and bless me with self-discipline in my studies. I pray in the name of the God who knows all. Amen.

This could cause some problems at home, Lord God. My family will not be happy with my grades because they know I can do better. I know I can do better too. The problem is how I feel about doing my work and studying for tests. You were so wise that You taught the teachers! But You also know how I feel. Help me to become a better student so I may use my full potential—to Your glory. In the name of the all-knowing Jesus, Amen.

FOR OTHERS

The day when grades come out finds my friends with many different emotions. Father, some of my friends work hard, but they never receive good grades. Other friends hardly work and they do well. Please send Your Holy Spirit Lord, first so that my friends know the most important thing: Your Son, Jesus, died to take away their sins. Then strengthen them to face parents who may be angry, or help them be humble, knowing You have given them the gifts that enable them succeed. Help them to work not only for grades but also for You. I pray in the name of God, who created all knowledge. Amen.

Tests

PREPARATION

Lord God, I need to study for a test now. As I begin to evaluate what I need to know, help me to have the right motivation for studying. Getting a good grade is important, but remembering important ideas and facts are even more important. That's where I sometimes have trouble. What is the use of learning things that will be on my test? Sometimes I don't see how I'll ever use this information. Help me with those doubts, Lord, so they don't stand in the way of my learning. Help me understand that perhaps something that seems useless today may become useful in the future. Settle my mind now, Lord. I'm ready to study. I pray in the name of the Lord who has plans for me in the future.

Amen.

JUST BEFORE

Heavenly Father, help me as I take this test. Empower me to do my best. Help me remember what I need, not only to receive a good grade but also to serve You and Your people. In Jesus' name. Amen.

RIGHT AFTER

I'm done, Jesus. The test seemed easy (hard). Help me, now that the test is over, to remember what You would have me know to better serve You. Thank You for passing the test I would be certain to fail—the test of how I might earn a place in heaven. Thank You for earning it for me through Your suffering, death, and resurrection. In Your name, Lord, I pray.

Amen.

Extracurricular Events

All that we have and are comes as Your gift, Father. Whether we win or lose, we belong to You. Whether we win or lose, we use the talents, skills, and physical abilities with which You have blessed us. Whether we win or lose, dear Father, help us to represent You, both in the way we play and in the way we act. Thank You for the most important victory ever won—the victory over our worst rivals—sin and Satan. We pray in Jesus' victorious name.   Amen.

ATHLETICS

Dear heavenly Father, I love to play
_____. Help me use the gifts You've
given me to glorify You. Help me to demonstrate good sportsmanship. Help me show that
You're the real Head Coach of my team. Lead me
to use my athletic experiences to demonstrate
both Your power of creativity and the love of
Jesus. May I do my best in Jesus' name.   Amen.

MUSIC

Thank You, dear Creator, for the gift of
music. Some people have found ways to use
music—like all Your gifts—as a tool for the
devil. Keep me from that evil, no matter how
tempting. Allow me to use music like the angels
did on the day Your Son was born. Help me hit
the right notes and keep the proper rhythm.
Let me remember that my notes flow from this
wonderful gift You gave me. My music is to
Your glory, Lord.   Amen.

DRAMA

Acting is important to me, Jesus. When I get nervous before the curtain rises, sometimes I wonder why I do this. But You have provided me with memory and a talent for portraying characters, and I use these gifts to Your glory now. Calm me; help me to play my role with imagination and accuracy. May the audience enjoy our performance and recognize our God-given gifts. It's only a play, Lord, but may it please You as much as it does the audience.

Amen.

forgiveness

FOR OTHERS

Now I know how hard it is to be merciful and gracious, dear Jesus. I know I'm obligated, as a Christian, to forgive others as I have been forgiven through Your suffering and death. Yet I have a hard time forgiving _____ for _____. Maybe it's the forgetting that gets in the way of forgiving. Give me the desire to forgive even though I fear I'll have trouble forgetting. Strengthen me to share Your mercy and grace. I pray in Your grace-filled name.

Amen.

Jesus, some of my friends are into things that don't please You. I'm praying for them because they are my friends. I know You suffered and died to take away the sins of the whole world and that You needed to do that only once. I also know that I can't pray that You forgive those who refuse to recognize or acknowledge their own sinfulness. But these people are my friends, Lord. Send Your Holy Spirit to them. Through Your Word, lead them to repentance, and give them power to resist the temptation that now enslaves them. I pray in Your merciful name. Amen.

FOR SELF

How amazing, dear Jesus, that a redeemed sinner like me can continue to sin! I guess I'm like the apostle Paul who admitted that although he knew right from wrong, he often did wrong. Yes, I am like that too. Forgive my sins once again, Jesus. Give me the willpower to eliminate my "favorite" sins—the ones I regularly commit. Keep me from falling to new sins that seem attractive. I thank You, Jesus. I'm confident that, as surely as I ask forgiveness, You have given it. Now I can go in peace. Amen.

Heavenly Father, I believe that I sin without even knowing that I've sinned. That's a weakness of human nature that baffles me. I ask Your forgiveness of those sins that I commit unknowingly. No, I'm not trying to excuse myself by pleading ignorance of the Law. You alone know how often I knowingly and unknowingly ignore Your Law. I know You love me, and I love You. I don't want anything to stand in the way of our relationship—including those sins of which I'm unaware. Thank You for Your love, so far-reaching that You forgive even those sins that extend beyond my consciousness. For Jesus' sake.

Amen.

I know Your sacrifice on the cross did everything necessary to make me a member of Your kingdom, Jesus. But here I am again. As much as I'm acquainted with Your mercy and grace, I still sin and need more of Your unconditional love. I know what I've done wrong, and I confess my sins to You now:_____. I hate my sins, Lord. Sometimes I don't hate them enough! Forgive me. Change my heart and my behavior. Thank You, Lord, for listening. Amen.

Sad Times

I am at a loss, Lord Jesus. Today, _____
_____.
My sadness probably is a small thing compared to all the sadness and suffering You see in the world. I remember the Bible stories about how Your unrepentant people made You feel and Your grief when a friend died. You know how I feel, and I know You care about me. I know You want me to be joyful and content, and I am firmly convinced that You love me, whatever

34

my mood. But I would like to be happier. If it is Your will, Lord, restore joy within me. Help me learn from my sadness to trust You as the only constant source of joy and peace.   Amen.

WHEN YOU ARE SAD BUT DON'T KNOW WHY

I can't explain it, dear Father. I'm not happy, but I don't know why. I guess it's natural sometimes to just be down and depressed. That's a consequence of sin, both mine and the world's. Cheer me with memories of what Jesus did for me on the cross. Give me joy like those first few people who saw Jesus raised on Easter. Help me think of others more than I think of myself right now. Cheer me, dear Father, for Jesus' sake.
Amen.

Relationships

You had friends, Jesus. There were the 12 who shared Your life and Your teachings so closely. There were others, too, like Mary, Martha, and Lazarus. You know how much fun friends can be. I have friends, Jesus. You're one of them, but I also have friends on earth. Thank You for placing others around me who like me and whom I like. Make our friendships strong and good. Help me remember that wherever I go with my friends, You are with us. Thanks for being my best Friend. Amen.

FRIENDS

Dear Jesus, allow me to see others who need my friendship. Please also place me in the company of those who would befriend me. Bless my friendships with Your presence. Use the bonds and fun we share to bring us closer to one another and closer to You. Guide my friends and me to be open to others, that we may accept new friendships without threatening old friendships. Thank You, Lord Jesus, for showing us how important good friends can be.   Amen.

LOSS OF A FRIEND

Lord God, I can't say whether I'm more angry or more hurt or more frustrated or more . . . more something! I lost a friend today. Maybe that's good; maybe that's bad. Only You know for certain. If it is Your will, Lord, restore our friendship. Make us as open to repentance and forgiveness for each other as You are for each of Your friends. If it is Your will that our close relationship not be restored, give me a forgiving heart and bless me with other friendships. I pray in the name of my most loyal Friend.

Amen.

Father, sometimes I feel so happy that I think even my toes are wriggling with laughter. But at other times, I feel insecure and uncertain, squirmy, if You know what I mean. I wonder about how to get along with him/her. I don't want to make him/her angry or disappointed. And I know that You have expectations for our relationship too. I ask You to bless our special friendship. Help us not to test Your will when it comes to sexuality. Although we may fall in love, let us always remember Your love for us. You know and want what is best. Your rules reflect what's best in how we treat each other, even when our emotions are swimming with affection. Guide us, Lord. Keep this special friendship both God-pleasing and fun for us.

Amen.

What does it take to be popular with the opposite sex, dear Jesus? Must I be drop-dead good looking? Must I be witty and charming, fragrant and zit-free? What if I'm not a good dancer or I can't wear the latest fashions? Okay,

okay—so I'm just shy, and I don't always think I'm likeable. Is there any hope for me? When it comes to friends, You are my best Friend. I know I can talk to You, sharing things like this. Give me confidence, dear Jesus, to know that Your Father created me to be me. He also created me for friendships with others—even of the opposite sex. Help me be satisfied with His creation, and lead me to the joy of those friendships that make me happy and glorify You.   Amen.

MALE-FEMALE RELATIONSHIPS

The word is sensitive, I know, dear Father. I'm often very sensitive about myself. I know just what makes me happy and angry. I know what I like and don't like. But I need Your guidance to know what others need. Male and female are quite different, as if I had to tell You! I have trouble with those differences, though, help me understand how to treat others as You created them to be treated. You gave Adam and Eve the best start ever by being their close Companion. Stay with me too, dear Father. Help me to be a good boyfriend/girlfriend, for Jesus' sake.   Amen.

I'm about ready to go out, Lord God. I'll be with _____. You created male and female to be friends, companions, and helpers for each other. I must confess, that sometimes I would rather that You weren't with me all the time. But I know You are here because You love me and know what's best. I'm sometimes tempted to cast aside Your guidance and commands in favor of how I feel when I'm with others of the opposite sex. I want them to think I'm liberated, independent, mature, and, well . . . cool. Don't let temptation get the best of me. Make me a leader, companion, and friend who follows You. And give us a good time too, Lord.   Amen.

I'm not getting along well at home, Lord. I would like more freedom, but it seems like I'm always treated as a child. Oh, I know I am a child—Your child and my parents' child. But I feel anything but childish—yet sometimes I'm made to feel that way. Is it because my parents love me so much that they want to keep me under their control? I pray that it is! Help me not to be a rebel. Help my parents to treat me according to my age and maturity and in accord with Your will. Never let them stop loving me!

Amen.

PARENTS

Give my parents and me the ability to talk reasonably with one another. Help us control our tempers and to freely forgive when offended. Strengthen us in knowing that You're part of the family too. Dear Father, You always know what is best—for children and their parents. Help us to see Your will and follow Your guidance. In Jesus' name.   Amen.

Dear heavenly Father, thank You for giving me a mom and dad who love me. They provide so much for me that I'm surprised I sometimes forget how grateful I am for their loving care. Help me to show my gratitude to You for them by being a godly (son or daughter). Strengthen us to face times of turmoil that surely will come. Help us to always remember that You gave my parents to me and that You gave me to my parents. Most important, help us to remember our Brother and Savior, Jesus, who took away our sins and empowered us to forgive one another.

Amen.

PARENTS

Help! Dear Father, when my parents fight, it frightens me. It makes me angry too. Why can't they get along? What will happen to me if they split up? Is their fighting my fault? Maybe I shouldn't ask so many questions when I talk to You, but I'm terribly upset by what is happening to my family. Take over, dear Father. Reconcile my parents to each other. Help me trust that You will take care of me no matter what happens. I put my future into Your loving hands, Lord Jesus.   Amen.

BROTHERS /SISTERS

Heavenly Father, sometimes I wish _____ could see You. Maybe he/she would treat me better. I know they love me, but sometimes it's hard to tell! I love him/her, but sometimes it's hard to tell that too. You made us a family, and I ask that You help us treat each other as family. Give us forgiving hearts and a short memory for each other's faults. Be with us always, and help us to grow in faith that we may serve You by serving each other. I pray in Jesus' name.   Amen.

Dear God, give me good teachers. Send teachers to our school who really care—about us and about You. Help me get along with my teachers and understand that they really represent You. If I disobey or misbehave, forgive me, and lead my teachers to forgive me too. Help me to be cooperative and open to what they teach. Help me also to make what they teach part of my life only when it agrees with Your Word. Send Your Holy Spirit to my teachers that they may serve You and give You glory through their teaching. If teachers are unfair or weak, help me to forgive them. Let all their teaching help me to better serve You and give You glory. I pray in the name of the Master Teacher. Amen.

Temptations

Wow! A few years ago I wouldn't have believed it possible to have such thoughts! You know, Father—about sex. It's everywhere—in books and magazines, on the Internet, at the movies, in music and videos, and it's found a curious corner in my own mind. Let me review for a moment, what I've learned about sex— from You. The most intimate sexual relationships are to be reserved for married couples. That sounds exciting and good, so much so that

I'm not sure I am able to wait for marriage. But give me power, Father, to conquer those urges that would take me beyond the boundaries that You want me to observe. Strengthen me, Father, to save sexual pleasures for marriage— the very reason you created such delight. For Jesus' sake. Amen.

CHEATING

Everybody does it, Lord Jesus. Cheating is such a temptation! Sometimes it's tempting because I don't study enough. Sometimes it's tempting because although I study, I still don't know all the answers. And grades are so important! Send your Holy Spirit to help me fight the urge to cheat. Help me to resist others as they seek to cheat. Give me the ambition I need to study well, and help me remember what I study. Thank You, dear Jesus, for not cheating as You worked to forgive my sins. You did it all. You did it completely. You passed the test—all for me. Help me to be more like You. Amen.

Oh, God, I know You know about anger. You were angry when Your people of the Old Testament refused to trust You. You were angry when they turned to other gods. You had every right to be angry. You have every right to be angry with me too. I sin often. My sins, together with the sins of the world, caused the suffering and death of Jesus. I'm sorry for that. And now I wonder if my anger is sinful. Your anger was always right and fair. Mine isn't always that way. Right now, I'm angry because _____. If my anger is fair, help me to forgive as You forgive me. If my anger is not fair, forgive me and help me seek forgiveness from anyone who has been hurt by my anger. Most of all, Lord, make me angry at sin and the devil. Let me hate both and seek only Your presence. In Jesus' name.   Amen.

Dear Jesus, I can't always have what I want. I know that You don't want me to steal. (You told me that in the Seventh Commandment.) Do store operators really get hurt when people shoplift? Doesn't their insurance cover theft and robbery? Yes, Lord, I know the questions only try to justify bad behavior. Stealing is sinful in Your sight, whether it's not returning too much change or slipping a CD inside a shirt. Make me content, Jesus, with what I have. You have given me everything I need for life. You also have given me everything I need for living with You in heaven. Thank You for all Your gifts. I especially thank You for the gift of eternal life. Send Your Spirit to always remind me that I have everything I need.   Amen.

Why is it that You allowed drugs into the world, Lord God? They surely provide lots of temptation, and they also ruin a lot of lives. Oh, I know, You didn't create drug abuse just to give me a hard time in hopes that I'll fall away. I know that illegal drugs are tools on the devil's workbench. He approves of anything that will hurt our bodies, break relationships, and give us a false and empty sense of happiness.

Of course, any problems, even problems with drugs, can bring people closer to You. Help those who abuse drugs to seek Your power in overcoming their dangerous habits. Give me stubborn strength to help my friends and me resist the temptation to use drugs, smoke or chew tobacco, or drink alcohol. Your Word says that my body is Your temple. Strengthen me to keep it clean and healthy. For Your sake.

Amen.

Peer Pressure

TO RESIST

How hard it must have been for You, dear Jesus, to avoid following the wrong friends. Thank You for resisting this temptation for me. When I want to go along with the crowd, when I feel I must do what they do to be accepted, send Your Holy Spirit to help me be myself. No, help me be something even better—help me be Yours! And as I follow You, help me also to lead others.　　　Amen.

I did it again, Lord Jesus. So often, I just feel like I need to belong to a group. I want to be popular, and I want to have fun with other kids my age. I know that some of their fun is actually sin disguised as a good time. Forgive me for following others when I should have followed You. Keep Your wonderful plans for me always in my mind. I know You want the best, and You will lead me if only I will follow. Make me a follower, dear Jesus. Yes, make me a follower who is always in Your company.   Amen.

Driving

I can't believe it, Father, I passed my test and have my license! Thank you for giving me the ability and the opportunity. Help me to be a careful driver; remind me of the responsibility that comes with being a licensed driver. Keep my passengers and me safe while we are on the road. For the sake of Jesus.   Amen.

BEFORE DRIVING

Lord God, I am about to start out on the road. I may only be going a few blocks or many miles, but I need You by my side. Help me to be a careful driver, remind me of the responsibility that I have on the road. Keep me safe from harm and danger. In Jesus' name.   Amen.

BEFORE RIDING ALONG

Dear Jesus, I am about to ride along with someone else. Allow me to be a good passenger. Keep me from distracting the driver from his or her task of being a careful and polite motorist. Allow us to safely reach our destination. Through Jesus, my Lord.   Amen.

Courage

GENERAL

Courage is a funny thing, Lord Jesus. Courage comes too easily at the wrong times. I guess I could earn a medal for bravery if it were given for sin. Often, I'm brave enough to defy You. I am bold when it comes to not loving others as You would have me love them. I'm pretty bold when it comes to not loving You either. I'm sorry, Lord. Give me real courage—the kind that comes from obedience to You. I need courage to defy the devil, my own sinful nature, and the sinful natures of my friends and family. Make me a brave soul, Lord. Thank You for Your courage that You demonstrated on the cross.

Amen.

I find it easy to say, "I love You" in the quiet of my prayers, dear Jesus. Nobody hears it but You. I want You to know that I really do love You, even though I'm kind of quiet about it with others. You see, sometimes I'm afraid what others might think of me if I proclaim my love too loudly or boldly. So many people around me just don't understand why anyone would love You, much less talk about it. I guess that's the problem though. Others don't know You like I know You. I need the courage to tell others how You took away their sins, just like You took away mine. I need the same power You gave to Moses when He was afraid to speak about You. Fill me with the Holy Spirit so I have the right words to say when opportunities to witness come my way. And thank You, Lord. Thank You for the courage to identify me and all sinners as Your forgiven children.   Amen.

Dear Jesus, You know about obstacles. Lots of people tried to keep You from accomplishing what the Father sent You to do. Yet, by the Father's power through the Holy Spirit, You overcame all challenges. Thank You for doing that, because I know You did it for me and other sinners.

I face challenges too. Many are the same challenges You faced at the hands of the devil. Unlike You, my own sinfulness presents obstacles to my well-being and happiness. Life can be so "un-fun" sometimes. Right now, here is what challenges me most:_____.
Let me face those challenges. With Your power, I too can overcome and succeed. Help me to know the kind of success that really pleases You.   Amen.

Success

Doesn't everyone ask You for success, dear Father? That's always been a big goal for people. Wasn't it Abraham who wanted to successfully father a child? And didn't King David want success over his enemies? Prophets, like Elijah and Isaiah, wanted to successfully lead their people to repentance. Sometimes You gave them the success they asked for; sometimes You didn't. Now I want success, Father. Yes, I'd like to be rich and popular—maybe even famous.

But I really want success on Your terms. Give me success in faith. Make me a successful disciple by what I say, think, and do. Thank You for not leaving this kind of success up to me and my skills and abilities. Thank You for taking away my sins so the Holy Spirit can fill me with spiritual success. That's the only kind I can take with me when I die! I pray in the name of Jesus.

Amen.

I hope You don't mind a hard question, God. Why are there as many successful unbelievers as believers? In fact, sometimes it seems that many more unbelievers are successful in life. How can that be? I thought You loved Your followers. Okay, You love everybody. But not everybody believes in You, so why do You bless them anyway?

You're not mad at me for asking, are You Lord? Maybe I already know the answer, but I don't like it. Is it that You bless everyone because You are patient and want all to believe in You? Is it because You want all people to be in heaven with You and Jesus and the Holy Spirit? Maybe I asked the wrong question.

Worldly success is Your gift. Some people mistakenly think they earn it. Help them to see what You have done for them. Help us all to recognize success as something You give so we can serve You better. Make me successful, God. And send the Holy Spirit to me so I always remember who deserves the credit. In the name of my Savior, Jesus.   Amen.

Miscellaneous Prayers for Others

This is hard, dear Jesus. You told us to love our enemies, and I'd like to try. But many of my enemies don't want my love or my prayers. I pray for them because You loved me when I was Your enemy. You died to pay for my sins, although I continue to sin. Give me a measure of Your grace that I too may love my enemies. Warm their hearts and souls with Your Word. Warm my heart and soul with Your Word too. I know that sometimes I am more enemy than friend, and I need Your forgiveness. I trust that You are the only one who can heal relationships that make friends of enemies. Bless me with that healing now, especially _____ . I pray in Your name.   Amen.

UNBELIEVERS

O Holy Spirit, I want what You want. You want everyone to be saved; therefore, You offer faith to all people. If Jesus returned today to end the world, I know millions of people would spend eternity in hell. I hardly can imagine what eternity is like, but burning in hell forever is horrible. Being apart from You and the Father and Jesus forever is even more horrible. Bring faith to all unbelievers. Be persistent and patient! Work powerfully through the Word of God to bring to faith Muslims, Buddhists, Mormons, Satanists, atheists, and all those without the Savior. I won't know how You choose to answer this prayer until I'm in heaven, but I trust Your mercy and power.   Amen.

Dear heavenly Father, You have given me a whole world for which to pray. Today's news stories once again tell of many suffering people. Please help all victims of tragedy and suffering, but especially _____who are in the news today. And so many people are in need of forgiveness. Send Your Holy Spirit to _____, calling for repentance and offering forgiveness. Sometimes the news is happy too. Today, I especially praise and thank You for_____. You are indeed a good God. I pray in Jesus' name.   Amen.

Daily Prayers

Father, You made Sunday a day of rest. I know Sunday is a day of worship too. I don't always feel like worshiping You, Lord. Sometimes I'd rather sleep in or do something else that I enjoy more. When I do worship You, often my mind wanders. The devil surely is busy with distractions! I love You, Lord, despite my inattention during worship. Create in me a clean heart, O Lord—one that worships You. In Jesus' name.   Amen.

Lord Jesus, it's off to school or off to work. I wish it were just off! Oh, I know You have blessed me with many things to do. Help me face this week with enthusiasm and encouragement. Give me a cheerful heart to face the many tasks required of me, and help me do well. In everything I do this week, help me do it to Your glory and according to Your will. For Jesus' sake.   Amen.

Thank You, dear God, for giving me another Tuesday. As I use the time You have given me, help me think of others who don't know Your love like I do. I need some ideas on how to show these people Your love through what I say and do. This Tuesday, I especially think of _____ who always seems in need of help. Help me be an answer to this prayer. Help me to act on my belief in Your concern and compassion for all people. Make me like Jesus in whose name I pray.   Amen.

WEDNESDAY

Happy Wednesday, Father! The middle of the week is a good opportunity to worship You—not just on Sunday. I praise You for all You've done—creating the world and populating it with people like me to take care of it and for using all Your power for my good. I especially thank and praise You for sending Jesus to take away my sins and for the Holy Spirit to help me grow in faith. I give thanks, Lord, for You are indeed good. In fact, You are the best. Keep me close to You forever. In my Savior's name.

Amen.

THURSDAY

It was a Thursday, dear Father, when Your Son, Jesus, met with His disciples to create what we now call the Lord's Supper. What a wonderful gift You gave them—and us—in Holy Communion. Each time I participate in the Lord's Supper, remind me of the forgiveness that Jesus earned for me. Remind me of the warm fellowship that Jesus had with those who believed in Him and the fellowship I have with other believers. For His holy name.   Amen.

Thank You God. It's Friday. Lots of people thank God it's Friday (TGIF, as some say), but I want to remember why I thank You. Yes, it's a good feeling to have the week behind me and the weekend ahead of me. But what makes Friday really great is that I remember what You did on Good Friday so long ago. Thank You for sending Jesus to suffer the punishment I deserve for my sins. Thank You for taking away my sins and leaving me with the sure promise of eternal life in heaven. Yes, thank You, God, for Friday. Let my life always celebrate this day—for the right reasons. For Your name's sake.   Amen.

Lord God, how easy to forget prayer on Saturday! This day seems to belong to me alone. But I really don't want it that way. I want You to be with me. During the week, it's easy to know how much I need You. Yet I also need You on those days away from school, work, and other events that so easily stress me. I need You today. As I get away from the weekday routines, bring me close to You. Help me see how You're always with me, just as You promise in the Bible. In Jesus' name.   Amen.

Birthday

Happy birthday to me! Thank You, Lord God, for making me ME. Now help me to give You glory and to serve You for as many birthdays as I will ever have. Thank You for parents who brought me into being. Thank You for friends and relatives who celebrate with me today. If it is Your will, Lord, give me many more birthdays. May You always be there to celebrate with me, Lord! In the name of the One who made me.

Amen.

It's a special day for someone special to me, dear Father. Thank You for bringing life to _____. Bless _____ with a strong faith and a heart to serve You. Be with us as we grow older together, and bless our relationship with joy and peace. If it is Your will, Lord, give _____ many more birthdays. I pray in the name of the Lord of life.   Amen.

Worship and Sacrament

You have once again brought me to the day of worship, dear Father. Give me the right attitude I need to tell Jesus and the Spirit how much I love them. Give me a clear voice for singing and a clear mind for praying. Although I'm not at worship for entertainment, open my heart to enjoy this opportunity for prayer and praise. Give me attentive ears and intellect, that I may hear Your Word and obey it. I look forward to the day when I'll be with all the Saints who praise Father, Son, and Holy Spirit in heaven. In Your most holy name.   Amen.

BEFORE THE LORD'S SUPPER

Thank You, Jesus, for inviting me to receive this miracle of Your holy meal. As I drink the wine, remind me that I really take the blood that You shed for me on the cross. As I eat the bread, remind me that I really take Your body, which You sacrificed to pay for my sins. I'm sorry that I brought this suffering on You. Strengthen me now through Your body and blood to hate sin and flee from it.   Amen.

BEFORE THE LORD'S SUPPER

Dear Savior, we come to Your table at Your gracious invitation to eat and drink Your holy body and blood. Let us find favor in Your eyes to receive this holy Sacrament in faith for the salvation of our souls and to the glory of Your holy name; for You live and reign with the Father and the Holy Spirit, one God, now and forever.

Amen. (*Lutheran Worship* p. 128)

Thank You, loving Savior, for bringing me to this Holy Communion with You. May my eating and drinking help me to be more like You. Make me forgiving, as You forgave. Place mercy in my heart, as mercy is in Yours. Give me power to withstand the temptations that seduce me. And make me one with all who know that You suffered, died, and rose to take away the sins of the world.   Amen.

Dear Lord Jesus, we thank and praise You that You have again refreshed us with the gift of Your holy body and blood in this comforting Sacrament. Bless our participation that we may depart from Your presence with peace and joy in the knowledge that we are reconciled to God. We ask this in Your name.

Amen. (*Lutheran Worship* p. 128)

Seasonal

Many poets have written about spring, but often they forget who gave it to us. Thank You, Father and Creator, for this new season of increasing daylight and the new life that comes with it. Thank You especially for bringing an eternal spring into my life. I know You love me and that You made me Your own. Spring is also the time of Easter—that best of all days in eternal history. Thank You for sending Jesus to save me. In His holy name I pray.   Amen.

SUMMER

Thank You, Father and Creator, for the seasons. I especially thank You today for summer. This season brings me time to relax, to change my pace. Fill my summer with happiness, but don't let my freedom tempt me to fall away from You. Let everything I see this summer remind me of what You have done here on earth. Let me especially remember how You sent Jesus to take away my sins. For His sake.

Amen.

FALL

Thank You, Father and Creator, for fall. You have provided so much diversity! In some areas, the leaves will change to bright colors, while other areas barely notice any change except the shorter daylight hours. Thank You, dear Father, for letting the light of Jesus shine on me and never allowing His love and care to diminish. Make me a light to others, reflecting Your changeless grace especially to those searching for answers to their changing lives. For the sake of my Lord and Savior.   Amen.

Thank You, Father and Creator, for winter. Although the days become darker, You fill the season with celebrations such as Christmas and the changing of the year. As I look forward to the winter holidays, also help me look forward to that time when You will send Jesus back to Earth. That party will last forever. All praise to You, Lord Jesus.   Amen.

ADVENT

Happy New Year, dear Father. We Christians get to celebrate a new year a whole month early! Our church recognizes Advent as a time to prepare for Jesus' second coming. I know it will be a surprise—that only You know when He will return. Thank You for giving me faith so I'm always ready for when He comes again. Help me use Advent to think about how my Savior was born into a humble human life, and how He suffered and died a most unspeakable death to pay for my sins. Now give me courage to wish others a happy new year as I witness to Your love and salvation. In Jesus' name.   Amen.

Many people think that this is the day when You first showered Your love on sinners, dear Father. Yet, I know that love began in the beginning—when You created the universe. You always had a plan for the good of people, even sinful people. We see that plan come to human life on Christmas. Help others to see what I see in Christmas. Help them to see beyond the decorated malls, the lights strung on houses, and images of Santa Claus and reindeer. Help them see their Savior, born to bring salvation to all. For Jesus' sake.   Amen.

NEW YEAR

Let the calendar always remind me of You, dear Friend. Some people have tried to do away with Your name, even wanting to remove it from those thousands of years B.C.—before You. Don't let that happen. Keep our knowledge of You fresh and alive in faith. Thank You for being in my life this past year. I especially thank You for _____. As I enter a new year, I'm especially concerned about _____. I know You will guide and help me. Thank You, Jesus.   Amen.

LENT

Why does Lent often seem so gloomy, Jesus? Oh, I know that Lent is the time we remember Your time on earth—how You taught and preached and performed miracles, how You suffered and died for our sins. Yes, that's the gloomy part. But I thank You for suffering, dying, and rising from the dead. You did that for me! I know the real reason we call Good Friday good! Praise to You, my Savior.   Amen.

You are risen, Lord Jesus! Thank You for defeating death and the devil for me and all sinners. Because You rose from the dead, I know that I too will rise after I die. Help me remember that my eternal life started when You sent the Holy Spirit to give me faith. Help me to live as Your faithful follower. Forgive me when I sometimes doubt Your love or find it hard to believe that incredible story of Your return to life. Send Your Holy Spirit to the whole world, that they too may know the secret of life forever with you.   Amen.

ASCENSION DAY

Lord Jesus, I wish I could have met You in person while You were on Earth. Your disciples wanted to keep You around too. The Bible reports how they gazed into the sky when You finally ascended into heaven after Your victorious life on earth. I know I'll see You face-to-face someday. Until that time, keep me satisfied with Your Word as You have left it for me in the Bible. Keep me satisfied with the Supper You began on the evening before You died for my sins. I know You'll come back. I can hardly wait to see You.   Amen.

PENTECOST

Today we celebrate Your giving birth to the Christian Church, dear Holy Spirit. We praise God for wanting all people to know what Jesus did for them. Yet many people still don't know. Work mightily through Your Word to bring faith to unbelievers. Use me as a missionary, even if my mission field is only my classroom or my home. As You once fed more than 5,000 people, feed the entire world with Jesus—the Bread of Life—in whose name I pray.   Amen.

Common Prayers

The Lord's Prayer

— sometimes known as the Disciples' Prayer because this is the prayer Jesus taught His followers.

TRADITIONAL VERSION

Our Father, who art in heaven, hallowed be Thy name, Thy kingdom come, Thy will be done on earth as it is in heaven. Give us this day our daily bread; and forgive us our trespasses as we forgive those who trespass against us; and lead us not into temptation, but deliver us from evil. For Thine is the kingdom and the power and the glory forever and ever.   Amen.

(Luther's Small Catechism with Explanation p. 16)

ALTERNATE VERSION

Our Father in heaven, hallowed be Your name, Your kingdom come, Your will be done on earth as in heaven. Give us today our daily bread. Forgive us our sins as we forgive those who sin against us. Lead us not into temptation, but deliver us from evil. For the kingdom, the power, and the glory are Yours now and forever.
Amen.

(Luther's Small Catechism with Explanation p. 16)

Prayers from Luther's Catechism

I thank You, my heavenly Father, through Jesus Christ, Your dear Son, that You have kept me this night from all harm and danger; and I pray that You would keep me this day also from sin and every evil, that all my doings and life may please You. For into Your hands I commend myself, my body and soul, and all things. Let Your holy angel be with me, that the evil foe may have no power over me.   Amen.

(Luther's Small Catechism with Explanation p. 30)

EVENING PRAYER

I thank You, my heavenly Father, through Jesus Christ, Your dear Son, that You have graciously kept me this day; and I pray that You would forgive me all my sins where I have done wrong, and graciously keep me this night. For into Your hands I commend myself, my body and soul, and all things. Let Your holy angel be with me, that the evil foe may have no power over me.   Amen. *(Luther's Small Catechism with Explanation* p. 31)

BEFORE MEALS

Lord God, heavenly Father, bless us and these Your gifts which we receive from Your bountiful goodness, through Jesus Christ, our Lord. Amen. *(Luther's Small Catechism with Explanation* p. 32)

AFTER MEALS

We thank You, Lord God, heavenly Father, for all Your benefits, through Jesus Christ, our Lord, who lives and reigns with You and the Holy Spirit forever and ever.   Amen.

(Luther's Small Catechism with Explanation p. 32)

Prayers
Based on the Commandments

COMMANDMENTS 1 – 3
A GOOD RELATIONSHIP WITH GOD

I pray to no stone statues, Father God, but I often think more highly of "things" than I think of You. And when it comes to expressing myself, sometimes I say words and think thoughts that I would never say if I saw You standing next to me. And then there is worship. It's so easy to find other things to do, even chasing the distractions in my mind when I'm attending worship services. For those sins, forgive me. Thank you for sending Jesus to give His whole self to me. Now help me give myself wholeheartedly to Him.   Amen.

COMMANDMENT 4

I call You Father, Lord God, and I mean it in the best way. Yet I often disobey You, even though You are King of kings, Lord of lords, and Father of fathers. I also disobey those whom You have given authority over me. Forgive my disobedience and give me a heart obedient to You and to all people You have provided to guide me. Bless and strengthen my parents, teachers, civil authorities, and others whom You want me to respect. Make them godly leaders of family, school, and government. Help them to show me Your love and mercy; help me to respect their wisdom and obey their rules.   Amen.

COMMANDMENT 5
LOVING OTHERS

Dear Jesus, You loved me so much that you suffered and died to pay for my sins. Knowing what You have done for me, help me share Your love with others. Some people are easy to love, and others . . . well, I know—You said love even my enemies. I can't do that without the Holy Spirit's help. So send the Holy Spirit to me that my love may reflect Yours. Empower me to fight hate, revenge, and contempt for others. Unite me with all who believe in You, that we may testify of Your grace and mercy.   Amen.

Jesus, You once told people that they sin with their thoughts as well as their deeds. That's so easy to do because it seems that no one can know a person's thoughts. And do jokes count as sin? You know, those jokes that refer to the body or to how people treat each other sexually? Yes, Lord, I'm sure that's just another way to disobey the sixth commandment. Forgive me, Jesus, for my sins of thought, word, and action. Give me healthy and wholesome relationships and friends who will help me fight temptation rather than seduce me with it. Thanks to Your constant forgiveness, I belong to You. Help me to live as You would have me live.   Amen.

COMMANDMENT 7
HONESTY

Dear Father, lies come way too easily. I remember the first lie ever spoken. It happened thousands of years ago in the garden that You gave to Adam and Eve. How many lies have You heard, dear Father? Even one was too many. And I must confess, I haven't always been honest either. In times when I'm tempted to cover up my guilt with a lie, help me remember that cover-ups hide nothing from You. Mostly, help me remember that You sent Jesus to take away my sins—that I need not cover up but confess my sins. In times when I'm tempted to cheat, help me remember that You didn't cheat when it came to taking away my sins. Your sacrifice was real. It changed my life. Make honesty a part of my life now as I go to serve You. For Jesus' sake.   Amen.

COMMANDMENT 8
WELL, WELL, WELL

I look forward to that day, dear Father in heaven, when Jesus will speak well of me before You. He will say that He knows me well, and that He, well, took away my sins. Then I'll get to live with You forever. Until that time, help me to follow Jesus' model. Help me to speak well of others, to try to understand behavior that seems strange or that angers me. Most of all, help me be as forgiving of others as You are of me. Whenever I talk about other people, make my mouth and my mind Yours. Give me courage and insight to defend others. Show me what is good about other people and remind me that You died to save all people, including people like me. In Christ Jesus, my Lord.   Amen.

Thank You, Father, for all that You have given me. Every good thing comes from You, and You always supply me with what I need for life. You even go beyond the "basics," bringing joy to my life with special gifts. Protect me from wanting more than I should have—from wanting more than what is good for me. Sometimes when I see what others have, I want their blessings too. Forgive me for not being content with Your gifts to me. Thank You for giving me Jesus. In the end, He is all that I need. He gives me a life that will never end. In the name of Christ.

Amen.

Miscellaneous Prayers

DOING GOD'S WILL

"Thy will be done." I say those words every time I say the prayer You taught Your disciples. I'm one of Your disciples too, dear Jesus. Sometimes, though, Your will is my won't! Forgive me when I disobey You—when I fail to love God and love other people as You love. Help me to know what You would have me do. Give me a desire to search out Your will in the Bible and as I hear Your Word elsewhere. Make Your will my will.   Amen.

SELF-CONTROL

Dear Father, I ask You to take away my "self"-control. When my self is in control, I often neglect how I should live as Your child. My "self"-control often leads me into sin. What I really need is for You to control me. Oh, I don't mean like a puppet or robot or anything like that. I mean control me with Your love. When I think of what You went through to take away my sins, I realize the depth of Your love. I want to return as much of Your love as I can. So control me Father. Make me just like Your Son.

Amen.

DECISION-MAKING

Dear Father, You have brought me a long way. You have helped me mature into greater ability to make decisions on my own. Of course, I know that I'm never completely on my own. You have given me Your Word, and I know it's the best guide to decision-making! Help me study Your Word regularly so I'm equipped for God-pleasing and wise judgment. Also help me to accept decisions that those in authority make for me. Sometimes I don't like those decisions.

Sometimes I feel like I'm treated like a child. But I also know that You send people into my life for the purpose of guiding me. I'm thankful for that, dear God, although I don't always show it. Continue to bless my life with Your supervision. In Your name I pray.   Amen.

PATIENCE

Dear Jesus, You are a model of patience. You were patient with Your disciples when they didn't understand You. And You're patient with me, although I'm often like those first disciples. You're patient with me even as I continue to sin. I need to have some patience, Jesus. I need patience especially when _____. In times of impatience, help me remember You. Make me merciful and gracious. Give me the peace that comes with patience. Yes, Lord, give me the patience of a saint, for that is what You have made me.   Amen.

Dear Father, You bless me through my country. I thank You for giving me a country in which I have the freedom to worship. But my country often ignores the blessings You have given it. Oh, I guess separation of church and state is a good idea—it protects us from being forced to worship false gods. But too often separation of church and state really becomes separation of God and country. In our freedom to worship, everyone's god gets equal treatment. Despite that, Your true Church continues to operate. Help it prosper so other citizens know how Jesus suffered and died to take away our sins and how He rose from the dead in victory over death and the devil.

Give us godly leaders who know what You have done for them and what You expect of them. Give them courage to stand on their faith and apply it to good government. Bring all people in this wonderful country to know You so they will live forever in an even more wonderful place! Through Christ Jesus, my Lord.   Amen.

I'm too busy, dear God. Slow things down. Never let me get so busy that I forget about You. Forgive my sins and strengthen me. Gotta go. Come with me Lord Jesus!   Amen.

8 9 10 11 12 13 14 15   18 17 16 15 14 13 12 11

ISBN 13: 978-0-7586-0035-6
ISBN 10: 0-7586-0035-6

9 780758 600356

Youth / Devotional / Prayer
06-1312

Concordia
Publishing House
www.cph.org